Jesus said, "I was [hungry and you] gave me food, I w[as thirsty and] you gave me something to drink, I was a stranger and you welcomed me, I was naked and you gave me clothing, I was sick and you took care of me, I was in prison and you visited me. Truly I tell you, just as you did to one of the least of these— you did it to me."

see Matthew 25: 35-36, 40

MW00387387

Mother Teresa of Kolkata
Saint among the Poor

Written and Illustrated by Didier Chardez

Foreword and Epilogue by Monsignor Leo Maasburg

Pauline
BOOKS & MEDIA
Boston

Library of Congress Control Number: 2016947616
CIP data is available.

ISBN 10: 0-8198-4958-8
ISBN 13: 978-0-8198-4958-8

The Scripture quotations contained herein are from the *New Revised Standard Version Bible: Catholic Edition,* copyright © 1989, 1993, Division of Christian Education of the National Council of the Churches of Christ in the United States of America. Used by permission. All rights reserved.

Originally published in German as *Mutter Teresa: Ein Licht für die Welt,* written and illustrated by Didier Chardez, Canisi Edition © 2016. All rights reserved.

Cover design by Mary Joseph Peterson, FSP

Translation copyright © 2016, Mary Leonora Wilson, FSP

English Edition copyright © 2016, Daughters of St. Paul

Prayer to Mother Teresa copyright © 2016, Daughters of St. Paul

Published by Pauline Books & Media, 50 Saint Pauls Avenue, Boston, MA 02130–3491

Printed in the U.S.A.

MTOK VSAUSAPEOILL7-1210063 4958-8

www.pauline.org

Pauline Books & Media is the publishing house of the Daughters of St. Paul, an international congregation of women religious serving the Church with the communications media.

1 2 3 4 5 6 7 8 9   20 19 18 17 16

CONTENTS

Foreword 1

People Dying on the Street 2

How It All Began..4

Longing for God 6

Convent Life Begins..8

Teacher and Principal.......................................10

Call within a Call 13

Waiting for Permission......................................16

Dressed in a Sari...18

Joining the Work 21

A House for the Dying 24

An Orphanage..26

Help for the Lepers..28

The World Discovers Mother Teresa 30

At the Vatican..32

Serving the Poor, Even in the Air......................37

Wartime Rescue 40

A Business Card 42

The Initials "MC"..44

A Typical Day 47

A Friend of the Pope..48

Rush to Canonization 49

So Many Children...51

Epilogue: Mother Teresa and the Power of Prayer.....................53

Prayer to Mother Teresa 56

FOREWORD

The Apostles spent three years on the road with Jesus the Master. I accompanied Mother Teresa on her many trips for seven years, partly because it was important to her to always have a priest with her. She didn't want to live a day without receiving Jesus at Holy Mass. She also wanted to make her confession every week, if possible.

She never spoke about it, but I was, in fact, her student during this time—I spent a long time in the school of a saint! Looking back, I am more and more aware of how much those countless experiences shaped my own spiritual life. As a priest, Mother Teresa drew me closer to Christ. I thank God for that.

The episodes in Mother Teresa's life included in this graphic novel have been illustrated especially for young people. This is how Mother Teresa would have wanted it. Not so much that you would come to know Mother Teresa herself better, but that through her you might better recognize God's work.

Everything Mother Teresa did, she did for her great love: Jesus Christ. She did everything hand-in-hand with him and through him. All the stories in this graphic novel are based on real events. And much of the dialogue is as I remember it. I am pleased that this book will be published for her canonization, and I hope that Saint Mother Teresa's life will touch many young people.

And for that, I ask God's blessing,

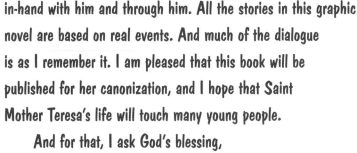

Monsignor Leo Maasburg worked with us on this graphic novel with great care and for a long time. Many stories in this book are his personal memories of the time he spent with Mother Teresa.

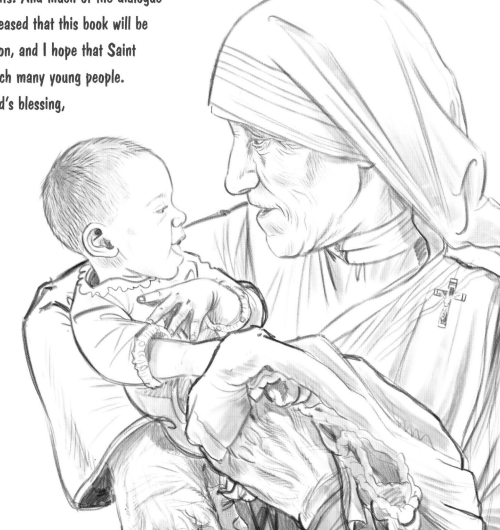

PEOPLE DYING ON THE STREET

KOLKATA, INDIA

EACH ONE OF THEM IS JESUS IN DISGUISE.

MISSIONARIES OF CHARITY
NIRMAL HRIDAY • ESTD -1952
MOTHER TERESA'S HOME FOR THE SICK AND DYING DESTITUTES

EVERY TIME YOU SMILE AT SOMEONE, IT IS AN ACTION OF LOVE, A GIFT TO THAT PERSON, A BEAUTIFUL THING.

I'VE LIVED MY ENTIRE LIFE ON THE STREET LIKE A STRAY ANIMAL. BUT NOW I'M DYING LIKE AN ANGEL.

HOW IT ALL BEGAN

FOR CENTURIES THE TURKS RULED MACEDONIA; CHRISTIANS WERE A MINORITY. ON AUGUST 26, 1910, AGNES GONXHE BOJAXHIU WAS BORN TO ALBANIAN PARENTS IN SKOPJE, MACEDONIA. SHE WAS BAPTIZED THE FOLLOWING DAY. ONE DAY AGNES WOULD BECOME KNOWN AS MOTHER TERESA.

HER FATHER, NICHOLAS, WAS A SUCCESSFUL BUSINESSMAN. HER MOTHER, DRANA, CAME FROM A RICH FAMILY.

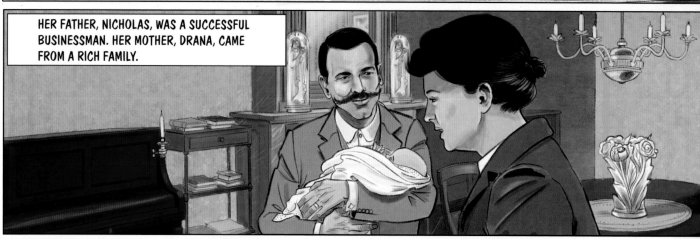

AGNES WAS THE YOUNGEST OF THREE CHILDREN. SHE HAD A BROTHER, LAZAR, AND A SISTER, AGA.

NICHOLAS WAS A BUILDING CONTRACTOR AND WAS THE ONLY CATHOLIC SERVING ON THE CITY COUNCIL.

TO PAPA NICHOLAS, HIS CHILDREN'S EDUCATION WAS VERY IMPORTANT. NOT EVERYONE IN THE OTTOMAN EMPIRE SHARED THIS VALUE AT THAT TIME.

WHEN YOU DO GOOD, IT'S AS IF YOU THREW A STONE IN THE WATER—IT RIPPLES AND FORMS WIDER AND WIDER RINGS.

AT HOME, MAMA DRANA TAUGHT THEIR CHILDREN ABOUT THE CATHOLIC FAITH.

MAMA DRANA ALSO SHOWED THEM HOW TO LIVE ACCORDING TO THE WORD OF GOD. EACH WEEK SHE VISITED THE SICK OF THE CITY AND TOOK THE CHILDREN ALONG WITH HER.

SHE OFTEN INVITED THE POOR TO EAT WITH THEM.

CHILDREN, INSIST THAT EVERY BIT OF THIS FOOD IS SHARED AMONG THE POOR.

IN 1919, JUST BEFORE AGNES' NINTH BIRTHDAY, PAPA NICHOLAS DIED UNEXPECTEDLY. AFTER THAT, MAMA DRANA WORKED AT HOME AS A SEAMSTRESS TO SUPPORT THE FAMILY.

LONGING FOR GOD

ONE SUNDAY, A MISSIONARY PRIEST PREACHED AT THEIR CHURCH. HE TOLD THE PEOPLE ABOUT HIS WORK IN INDIA. AGNES FELT A BURNING DESIRE TO SERVE GOD.

AGNES HAD MANY TALENTS. SHE ENJOYED ACTING AND PLAYING THE MANDOLIN . . .

. . . SHE ALSO READ A LOT AND FOUND JOY IN THE QUIET MOMENTS SHE TOOK TO THINK AND PRAY.

BY THE TIME SHE WAS TWELVE, AGNES KNEW THAT SHE WANTED TO GIVE HER LIFE TO JESUS. BUT HOW?

THE INFLUENCE OF THE JESUIT PRIEST, FATHER FRANJO JAMBREKOVIC, WAS VERY IMPORTANT AT THIS TIME IN AGNES' LIFE.

AGNES LISTENED CLOSELY TO FATHER FRANJO'S PREACHINGS AND SPOKE OFTEN WITH HIM ABOUT JESUS CHRIST, THE CHURCH, THE SAINTS, AND THE MISSIONS.

FATHER, HOW DO PEOPLE KNOW GOD'S PLAN FOR THEIR LIVES?

FROM THE JOY THEY FEEL, MY CHILD, FROM THE JOY!

AFTER A PILGRIMAGE, AGNES FELT A CLEAR DESIRE TO CONSECRATE HER LIFE TO GOD.

SO, AGNES, YOU WANT TO ENTER THE COMMUNITY OF THE SISTERS OF LORETO AND BE PART OF THEIR TEACHING MISSION?

BUT WHY, AGNES?

LAZAR, WHEN GOD CALLS, WE SHOULDN'T RESIST THE INVITATION.

ON SEPTEMBER 25, 1928, EIGHTEEN-YEAR-OLD AGNES LEFT HER FAMILY AND TRAVELED TO LIVE WITH THE SISTERS OF LORETO IN IRELAND. SHE WORE A TAG WITH HER NAME AND DESTINATION WRITTEN ON IT.

AGNES ENTERED THE CONVENT OF THE MISSIONARY SISTERS OF OUR LADY OF LORETO NEAR DUBLIN, IRELAND.

CONVENT LIFE BEGINS

THERE SHE LEARNED ENGLISH . . .

. . . PRAYED MUCH AND READ THE BIBLE.

SHE ALSO BECAME FAMILIAR WITH THE SPIRITUAL EXERCISES OF SAINT IGNATIUS OF LOYOLA.

THESE "EXERCISES" ARE PRACTICED IN SILENCE. THEY ARE TOOLS OF DISCERNMENT AND HELP ONE TO RECOGNIZE GOD'S WILL FOR HIS OR HER LIFE.

AFTER SOME MONTHS AGNES WAS SENT TO INDIA. LATER SHE WROTE THAT EVER SINCE SHE HAD RECEIVED JESUS FOR THE FIRST TIME IN HOLY COMMUNION, A LOVE FOR SOULS HAD BEEN BURNING IN HER.

AGNES WAS SHOCKED BY THE POVERTY SHE ENCOUNTERED. SICK AND HOMELESS PEOPLE LAY IN THE MIDDLE OF THE STREET. MANY DIED.

THESE PEOPLE HAD ABSOLUTELY NOTHING, EXCEPT HUNGER, SICKNESS AND MISERY.

AGNES TRAVELED TO DARJEELING. THERE SHE BEGAN HER NOVITIATE.*

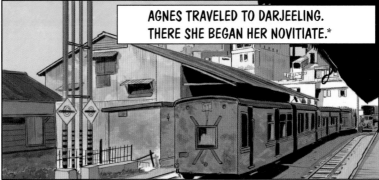

DURING THIS TIME, THE OLDER SISTERS TAUGHT AGNES ABOUT HOW TO GIVE ALL OF HERSELF TO JESUS.

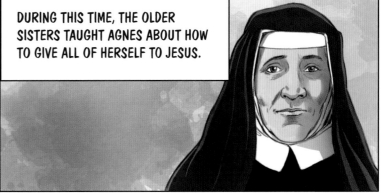

9

* The beginning stage of becoming a religious sister, brother, or priest

TEACHER AND PRINCIPAL

FULL OF JOY, IN MAY OF 1931, AGNES PROFESSED HER FIRST VOWS OF POVERTY, CHASTITY, AND OBEDIENCE.

SHE CHOSE THE NAME MARY TERESA, IN HONOR OF SAINT THÉRÈSE OF LISIEUX . . .

. . . A CARMELITE NUN, WHO WAS CANONIZED IN 1925 AND MADE PATRONESS OF THE MISSIONS.

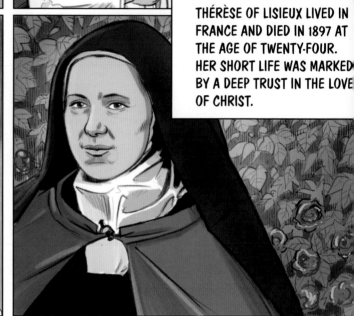

THÉRÈSE OF LISIEUX LIVED IN FRANCE AND DIED IN 1897 AT THE AGE OF TWENTY-FOUR. HER SHORT LIFE WAS MARKED BY A DEEP TRUST IN THE LOVE OF CHRIST.

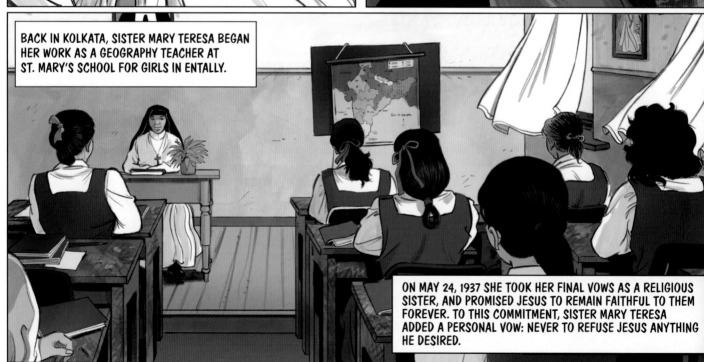

BACK IN KOLKATA, SISTER MARY TERESA BEGAN HER WORK AS A GEOGRAPHY TEACHER AT ST. MARY'S SCHOOL FOR GIRLS IN ENTALLY.

ON MAY 24, 1937 SHE TOOK HER FINAL VOWS AS A RELIGIOUS SISTER, AND PROMISED JESUS TO REMAIN FAITHFUL TO THEM FOREVER. TO THIS COMMITMENT, SISTER MARY TERESA ADDED A PERSONAL VOW: NEVER TO REFUSE JESUS ANYTHING HE DESIRED.

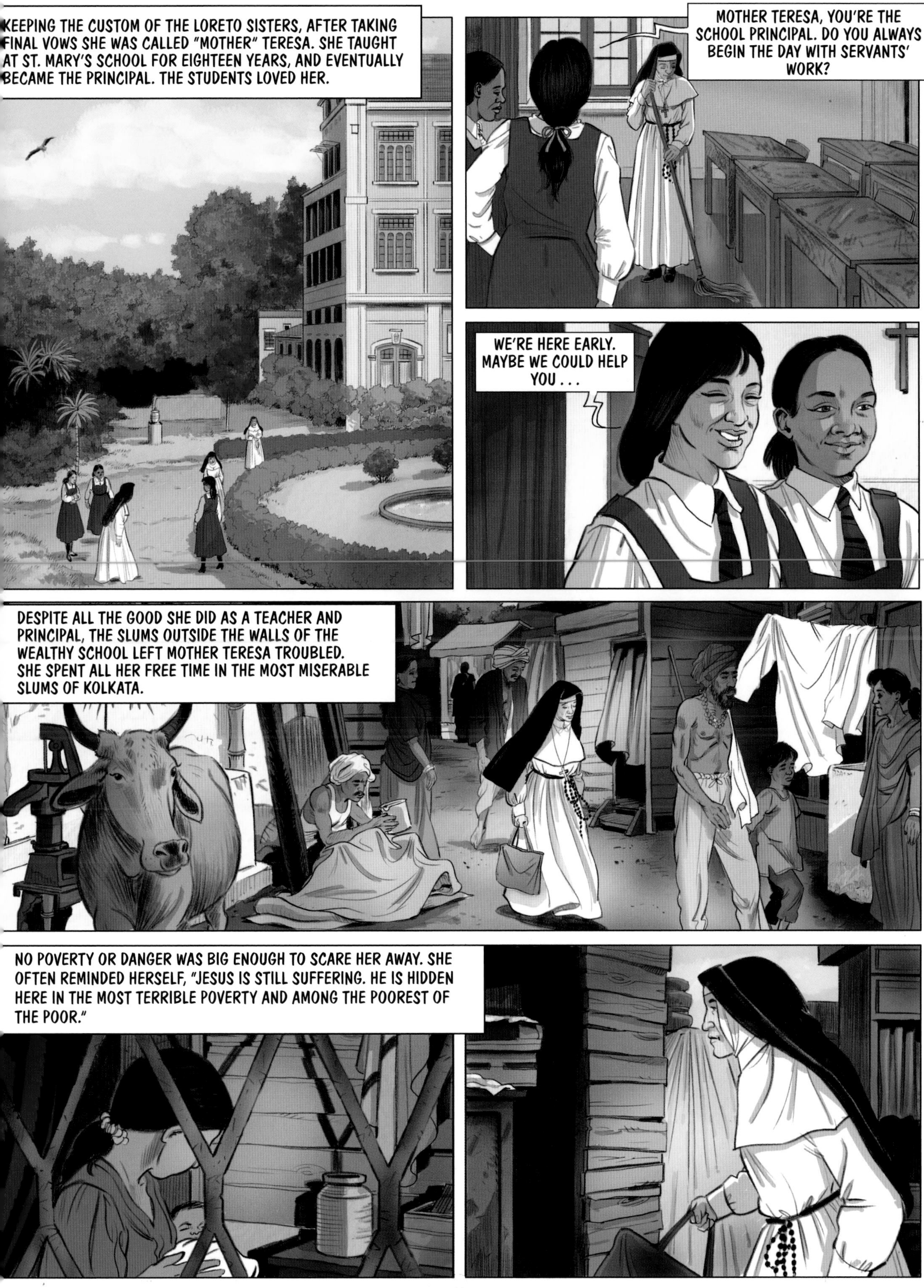
KEEPING THE CUSTOM OF THE LORETO SISTERS, AFTER TAKING FINAL VOWS SHE WAS CALLED "MOTHER" TERESA. SHE TAUGHT AT ST. MARY'S SCHOOL FOR EIGHTEEN YEARS, AND EVENTUALLY BECAME THE PRINCIPAL. THE STUDENTS LOVED HER.
MOTHER TERESA, YOU'RE THE SCHOOL PRINCIPAL. DO YOU ALWAYS BEGIN THE DAY WITH SERVANTS' WORK?
WE'RE HERE EARLY. MAYBE WE COULD HELP YOU . . .
DESPITE ALL THE GOOD SHE DID AS A TEACHER AND PRINCIPAL, THE SLUMS OUTSIDE THE WALLS OF THE WEALTHY SCHOOL LEFT MOTHER TERESA TROUBLED. SHE SPENT ALL HER FREE TIME IN THE MOST MISERABLE SLUMS OF KOLKATA.
NO POVERTY OR DANGER WAS BIG ENOUGH TO SCARE HER AWAY. SHE OFTEN REMINDED HERSELF, "JESUS IS STILL SUFFERING. HE IS HIDDEN HERE IN THE MOST TERRIBLE POVERTY AND AMONG THE POOREST OF THE POOR."

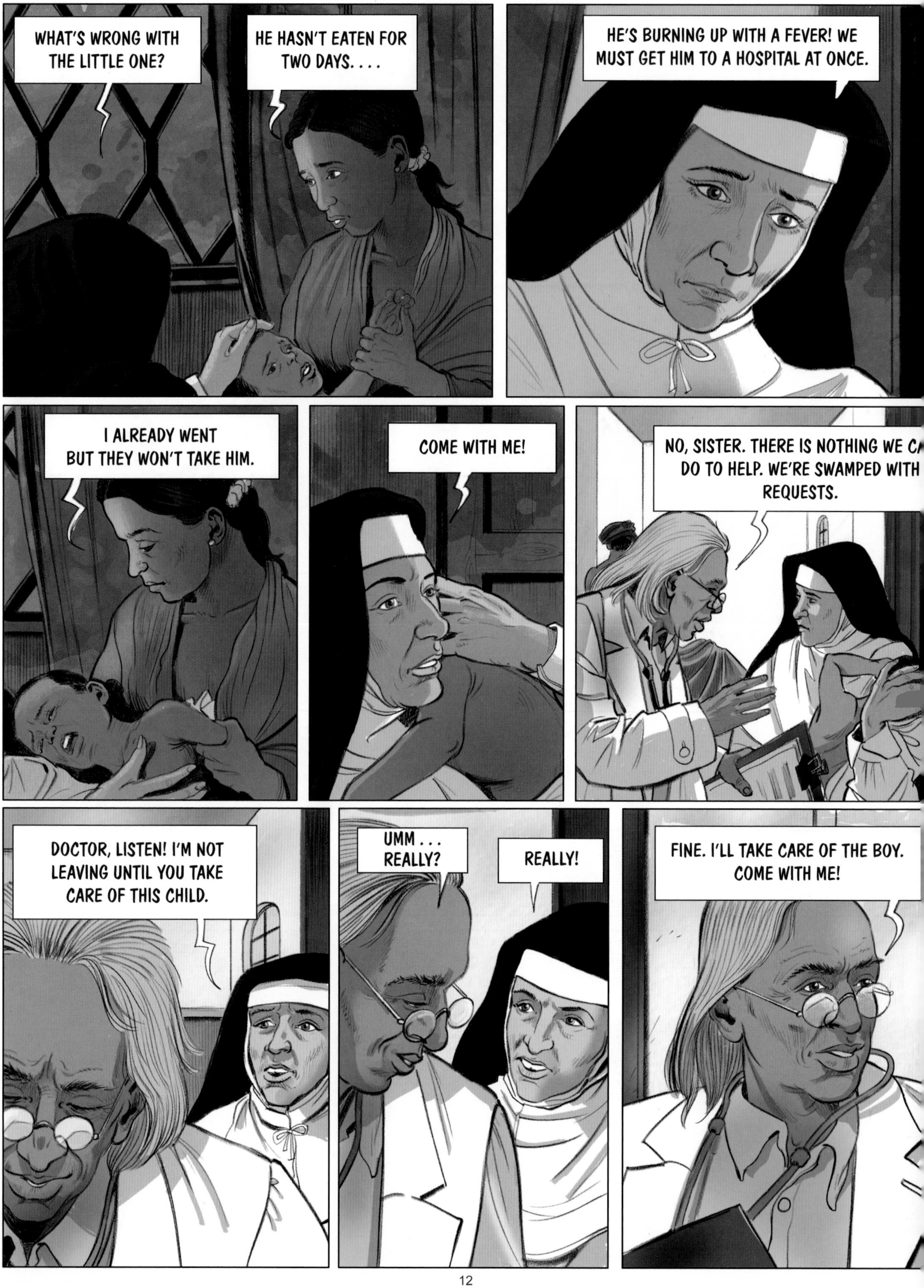
WHAT'S WRONG WITH THE LITTLE ONE?
HE HASN'T EATEN FOR TWO DAYS. . . .
HE'S BURNING UP WITH A FEVER! WE MUST GET HIM TO A HOSPITAL AT ONCE.
I ALREADY WENT BUT THEY WON'T TAKE HIM.
COME WITH ME!
NO, SISTER. THERE IS NOTHING WE CA DO TO HELP. WE'RE SWAMPED WITH REQUESTS.
DOCTOR, LISTEN! I'M NOT LEAVING UNTIL YOU TAKE CARE OF THIS CHILD.
UMM . . . REALLY?
REALLY!
FINE. I'LL TAKE CARE OF THE BOY. COME WITH ME!

A CALL WITHIN A CALL

YEARS PASSED. . . . ON SEPTEMBER 10, 1946, MOTHER TERESA SET OUT FOR HER YEARLY RETREAT.

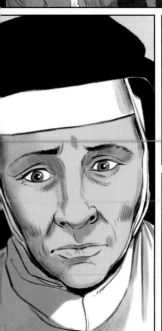

EVERYWHERE SHE SAW PEOPLE IN NEED, EVEN AT THE TRAIN STATION.

DURING THE TRAIN RIDE SHE HEARD A DISTINCT VOICE. IN IT, SHE RECOGNIZED WHAT SHE WOULD LATER SAY WAS HER "CALL WITHIN A CALL."

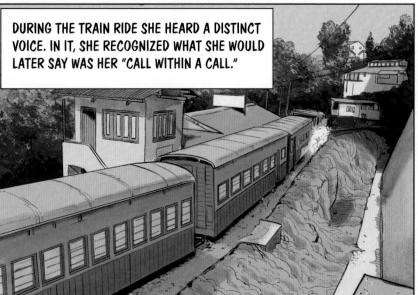

IT WAS NOT AN APPARITION. IT WAS A MESSAGE FROM GOD TELLING HER WHAT HE WANTED HER TO DO.

THE MESSAGE WAS VERY CLEAR. GOD WANTED HER TO BE POOR HERSELF AND TO LOVE HIM IN THE POOREST OF THE POOR.

MOTHER TERESA WAS AWARE THAT THE LORETO SISTERS DID NOT MINISTER IN THE SLUMS. SHE WOULD HAVE TO LEAVE THEM TO BEGIN HER OWN WORK. BUT HOW?

ON THIS "INSPIRATION DAY" SHE EXPERIENCED GOD'S LOVE.

SHE HEARD JESUS' WORDS ON THE CROSS, "I THIRST."

WHEN JESUS SAID, "I THIRST," IT WAS HIS WAY OF SAYING, "I LOVE YOU AND I DESIRE YOUR LOVE."

AS LONG AS PEOPLE DON'T KNOW THAT JESUS THIRSTS FOR THEM, THEY CAN'T UNDERSTAND HIM.

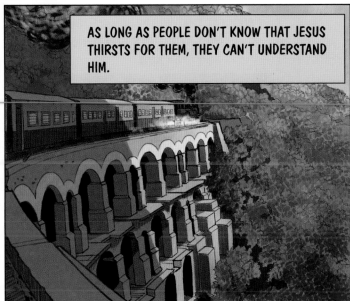

MOTHER TERESA HEARD JESUS SAY CLEARLY TO HER: "COME, BRING ME TO THE POOR, AND INTO THE DARK HOLES WHERE YOU FIND THEM. COME, AND BE MY LIGHT."

WAITING FOR PERMISSION

MOTHER TERESA CARRIED THIS EXPERIENCE IN HER HEART.

BACK IN KOLKATA SHE CONFIDED IN HER SPIRITUAL DIRECTOR, A BELGIAN JESUIT NAMED FATHER VAN EXEM. SHE EXPLAINED TO HIM THAT SHE FELT GOD WAS ASKING HER TO DO SOMETHING DIFFERENT.

I SUGGEST THAT YOU PRAY MUCH, BUT KEEP QUIET ABOUT THIS EXPERIENCE FOR NOW.

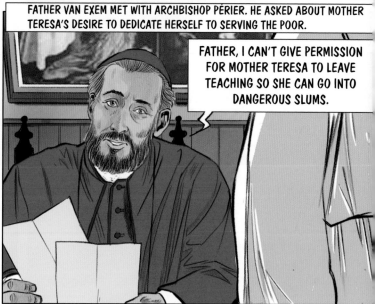

FATHER VAN EXEM MET WITH ARCHBISHOP PÉRIER. HE ASKED ABOUT MOTHER TERESA'S DESIRE TO DEDICATE HERSELF TO SERVING THE POOR.

FATHER, I CAN'T GIVE PERMISSION FOR MOTHER TERESA TO LEAVE TEACHING SO SHE CAN GO INTO DANGEROUS SLUMS.

SO BE IT, YOUR EXCELLENCY! WITHOUT OBEDIENCE THERE IS NO BENEFIT.

THANK YOU, FATHER, I'M NOT SURPRISED BY THE BISHOP'S ANSWER. SO, I WILL OBEY AND PRAY MORE.

IF JESUS WANTS THIS WORK, HE WILL FIND A WAY FOR ME TO DO IT.

MOTHER TERESA BECAME SERIOUSLY ILL.

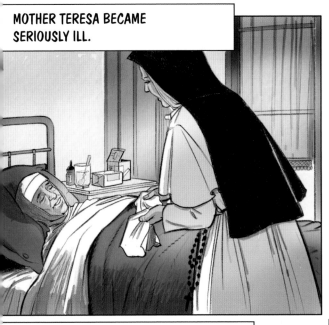

SHE OFFERED UP HER SUFFERING AND PRAYED: "JESUS MAY YOUR WILL BE DONE WITH ME AND IN ME."

SHE PRAYED A GREAT DEAL ABOUT ARCHBISHOP PÉRIER'S ANSWER. IN TIME SHE RECOVERED AND CAME TO ACCEPT . . .

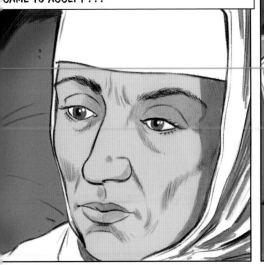

. . . THAT THE ARCHBISHOP DENIED HER REQUEST BECAUSE HE WANTED TO KEEP HER SAFE FROM THE VIOLENT OUTBURSTS BETWEEN INDIANS AND PAKISTANIS AT THE TIME.

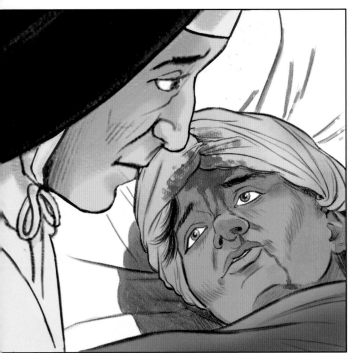

AFTER A YEAR AND A HALF, ARCHBISHOP PÉRIER DECIDED IT WAS TIME TO ASK CHURCH LEADERS IN ROME IF MOTHER TERESA COULD LEAVE THE LORETO SISTERS AND BEGIN HER WORK AMONG THE POOR.

DRESSED IN A SARI*

KOLKATA, AUGUST 1948

MOTHER TERESA! THE GENERAL SUPERIOR IS ASKING FOR YOU!

YOU CALLED ME, MOTHER?

YES, SISTER TERESA, WE HAVE NEWS FROM ROME.

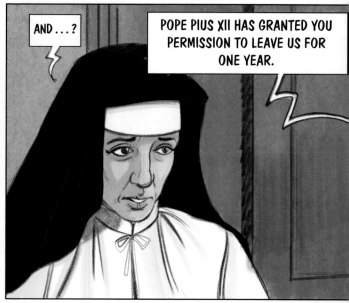

AND . . . ?

POPE PIUS XII HAS GRANTED YOU PERMISSION TO LEAVE US FOR ONE YEAR.

NOW YOU CAN DEDICATE YOURSELF TO WORKING AMONG THE POOR. PERHAPS YOU WILL FOUND A NEW ORDER.

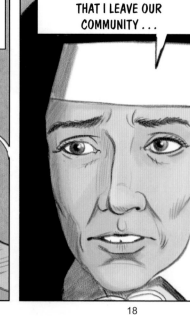

IT'S WITH A HEAVY HEART THAT I LEAVE OUR COMMUNITY . . .

YOU ARE BEING CALLED TO SOMETHING ELSE. GOD WILL LEAD YOU.

*Traditional garment worn by the women of India

SO YOU'RE LEAVING US TODAY . . .

ARE YOU GOING TO WEAR A SARI NOW?

I WANT TO SERVE THE POOR HERE IN KOLKATA. THEY DRESS LIKE THIS.

BUT FIRST I'M GOING TO PATNA TO LEARN HOW TO CARE FOR THE SICK.

DO YOU HAVE ENOUGH MONEY FOR THE TRIP?

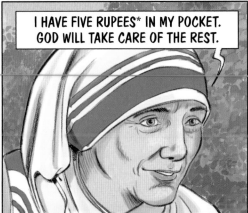

I HAVE FIVE RUPEES* IN MY POCKET. GOD WILL TAKE CARE OF THE REST.

* A rupee is Indian money. At that time, five rupees would equal about one US dollar.

FOUR MONTHS LATER, MOTHER TERESA RETURNED TO KOLKATA. SHE BEGAN TO WRITE DOWN HER THOUGHTS AND EXPERIENCES IN HER DIARY.

Extreme poverty robs people of their humanity.

MOTHER TERESA BEGAN HER WORK BY TEACHING CHILDREN IN THE SLUMS TO READ AND WRITE.

A for Apple
B for Bat
C for Cat
D for Dog

WHEN SHE RECEIVED FOOD, MOTHER TERESA GAVE MOST OF IT AWAY TO THE CHILDREN.

I HAVE SO MANY STUDENTS THAT I CAN'T CONTINUE TO TEACH LESSONS ON THE STREETS. EVERY DAY THERE ARE NEW STUDENTS, FATHER VAN EXEM.

YOUR WORK IS VERY IMPORTANT. LET'S SEE IF WE CAN FIND A PROPER PLACE FOR CLASSES.

IN TILJALA, I SAW A PLACE THAT COULD WORK. TELL THE OWNER THAT I SENT YOU.

JOINING THE WORK

ONE NIGHT . . .

SUBHASINI*?

YES!

WHAT ARE YOU DOING HERE SO LATE IN THE EVENING?

NOTHING. I JUST WANTED TO SEE . . .

SEE WHAT?

WHAT YOU'RE DOING...

BUT . . .

I'VE THOUGHT ABOUT IT FOR A LONG TIME! I WANT TO GO WITH YOU.

I WANT TO SERVE THE POOR, TOO. I FEEL GOD IS CALLING ME TO DO THE SAME THING YOU'RE DOING!

*Subhasini was a former student of Mother Teresa's at St. Mary's School. She became the first to join Mother Teresa's new order.

THIS BUILDING IS WONDERFULLY SUITED TO YOUR WORK, DON'T YOU THINK?

MOTHER TERESA, WE COULD CARE FOR THE SICK HERE.

FORTY RUPEES A MONTH IS TOO MUCH!

BUT, THAT'S A STANDARD PRICE.

HOW CAN I PAY SO MUCH RENT? I DON'T HAVE THE MONEY!

OKAY, FINE! HOW MUCH CAN YOU PAY?

THAT DEPENDS ON HOW MUCH THE RENOVATIONS WILL COST.

HMM . . . I THINK AT LEAST 1,500 RUPEES.

BUT WITH THE SUPPORT THAT YOU HAVE, YOU COULD RENOVATE THE BUILDING FOR FREE.

WHAT SUPPORT?

THEM! YOUR FORMER STUDENTS.

GOOD AFTERNOON, MOTHER TERESA! WE'RE GRADUATING . . .

. . . AND NOW WE WANT TO WORK WITH YOU AND SERVE JESUS IN THE POOREST OF THE POOR.

!

ON OCTOBER 7, 1950, THE CONGREGATION OF THE MISSIONARIES OF CHARITY WAS FOUNDED. THE NEW COMMUNITY GREW VERY QUICKLY.

1950

THE MAN WHO WAS HERE, WHERE IS HE?

HE'S DEAD . . .

A HOUSE FOR THE DYING

DEAD? DID HE DIE HERE ALL ALONE ON THE STREET?

YES. I SAW SOME MEN CARRY HIM AWAY.

JESUS, GIVE US A PLACE WHERE PEOPLE WHO HAVE INCURABLE ILLNESSES CAN DIE WITH DIGNITY AND LOVE.

THE MAYOR OF KOLKATA GAVE MOTHER TERESA A BUILDING. IT WAS NEXT TO THE TEMPLE OF THE HINDU GODDESS, KALI. HERE THE FIRST HOSPICE* WAS BUILT.

BUT THE HINDUS FELT OFFENDED WHEN THEY FOUND OUT THAT CHRISTIANS WERE WORKING SO CLOSE TO THEIR TEMPLE. THEY THREATENED TO USE VIOLENCE TO STOP THE SISTERS.

*Hospice is care for the dying.

24

DON'T EVER COME BACK HERE AGAIN!

BUT WHY?

THIS PLACE IS SACRED TO US HINDUS!

GO AWAY AND STOP PUSHING YOUR RELIGION ON OTHERS!

NO MATTER WHAT RELIGION THEY WERE, HOSPICE PATIENTS WERE CARED FOR WITH LOVE.

BUT THE HINDUS DID NOT KNOW THAT, UNTIL ONE DAY . . .

. . . ONE OF THE LOCAL LEADERS WENT INSIDE TO SEE WHAT WAS HAPPENING. HE CHANGED HIS MIND WHEN HE SAW WITH HIS OWN EYES THE GOOD WORK THE SISTERS WERE DOING.

I'LL DO WHAT YOU WANT AND SEND MOTHER TERESA AWAY, BUT ONLY WHEN YOUR MOTHERS AND SISTERS COME HERE TO CARRY ON THE WORK THESE WOMEN ARE DOING.

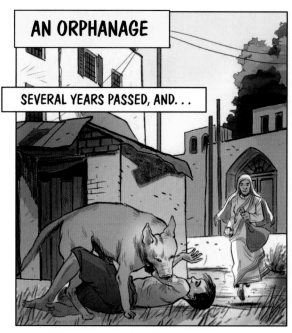

AN ORPHANAGE

SEVERAL YEARS PASSED, AND. . .

MOTHER TERESA SAW THAT SICK AND DYING PEOPLE WERE NOT THE ONLY ONES WITH NEEDS. THERE WERE ALSO MANY CHILDREN WITH NO ONE TO CARE FOR THEM.

MOTHER, THE BOY YOU BROUGHT US IS DEAD. . . .

WE MUST GIVE ORPHANS LIKE HIM A HOME, OR MORE WILL DIE.

IN 1955 THE MISSIONARIES OF CHARITY'S FIRST ORPHANAGE, NIRMALA SHISHU BHAVAN*, WAS OPENED IN KOLKATA. MOTHER TERESA RELIED COMPLETELY ON GOD'S HELP TO MAKE IT A REALITY.

CHILDREN, WE HAVE ENOUGH FOOD FOR THE NEXT FEW DAYS. WE WILL TRUST GOD TO PROVIDE AFTER THAT.

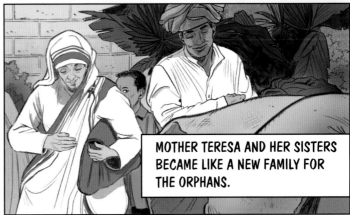

MOTHER TERESA AND HER SISTERS BECAME LIKE A NEW FAMILY FOR THE ORPHANS.

WHO WOULD LIKE SOME FRUIT?

*Nirmala Shishu Bhavan means Children's Home of the Immaculate Heart.

HELP FOR THE LEPERS

LEPROSY IS A DISEASE THAT CAUSES SKIN SORES, NERVE DAMAGE, AND MUSCLE WEAKNESS.

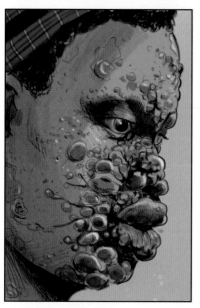

BECAUSE PEOPLE WERE AFRAID OF CATCHING THIS PAINFUL ILLNESS, LEPERS WERE OFTEN OUTCAST FROM THE COMMUNITY. THEY WERE LEFT ALONE AND NO ONE TOOK CARE OF THEM.

MOTHER TERESA LOVED AND CARED FOR THE LEPERS. SHE SAID: TO GOD, THEY ARE VERY BEAUTIFUL PEOPLE. IF THEY HAVE LEPROSY, GOD DOES NOT TURN HIS BACK ON THEM. HE DRAWS THESE PEOPLE CLOSER TO HIMSELF. WE MUST DO THE SAME.

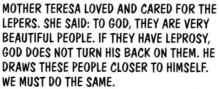

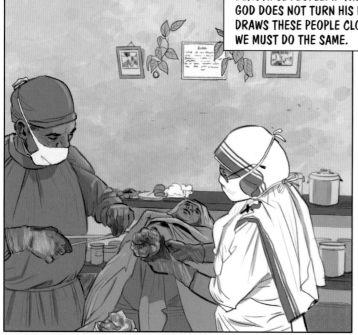

1957, MOTHER TERESA DECIDED TO OPEN CENTER FOR LEPERS. BUT THERE WAS A LOT OF RESISTANCE FROM OTHER PEOPLE.

MOTHER TERESA UNDERSTOOD THEIR CONCERNS.

THEY'RE AFRAID OF CATCHING LEPROSY.

WHEREVER WE GO, WE'LL HAVE THE SAME PROBLEM.

I HAVE AN IDEA. MAYBE WE CAN USE MOBILE CLINICS.

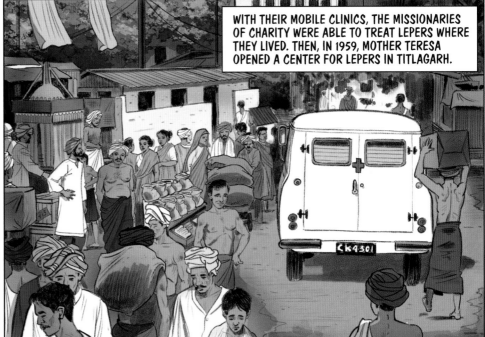

WITH THEIR MOBILE CLINICS, THE MISSIONARIES OF CHARITY WERE ABLE TO TREAT LEPERS WHERE THEY LIVED. THEN, IN 1959, MOTHER TERESA OPENED A CENTER FOR LEPERS IN TITLAGARH.

MOTHER TERESA WORKED HARD TO SERVE AND CARE FOR THE POOR. DURING THIS TIME SHE ENDURED THE PAIN OF FEELING SAD AND REJECTED BY GOD.

THIS CAN HAPPEN TO ANYONE, EVEN THE SAINTS. SOMETIMES IT IS CALLED A "DARK NIGHT OF THE SOUL." MOTHER TERESA WROTE TO HER CONFESSOR ABOUT NOT FEELING GOD'S LIGHT AND INSPIRATION.

FOR MOTHER TERESA, THIS DARKNESS LASTED FIFTY-FOUR YEARS. DESPITE THIS SPIRITUAL STRUGGLE, SHE CONTINUED IN THE WORK GOD CALLED HER TO DO.

THE WORLD DISCOVERS MOTHER TERESA

THE MEDIA BECAME MORE AND MORE AWARE OF THE WORK THAT THE MISSIONARIES OF CHARITY WERE DOING. SOON MOTHER TERESA AND HER SISTERS WERE FAMOUS ALL OVER THE WORLD.

BY 1964, THE SISTERS HAD DOZENS OF HOUSES IN INDIA. SOON THE ORDER BEGAN WORKING IN OTHER COUNTRIES, STARTING IN VENEZUELA...

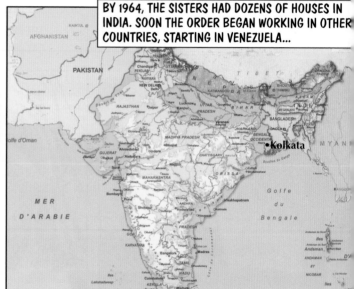

NOT EVERYONE, THOUGH, WANTED TO LISTEN TO MOTHER TERESA. HER MESSAGE WAS CHALLENGING THOSE WHO PLACED TOO MUCH IMPORTANCE ON COMFORT AND MATERIAL WEALTH.

STILL HER WORK AMONG THE POOR WA[S] RECOGNIZED. IN 1962, THE PRESIDENT OF INDIA PRESENTED HER WITH THE PADMASHRI AWARD* FOR HER WORK IN THE SLUMS.

*The Padmashri Award is given for distinguished service in any field.

...CAUSE MOTHER TERESA WAS SO HUMBLE, ALL THE ATTENTION ...E MEDIA BROUGHT HER MADE HER UNCOMFORTABLE.

MOTHER TERESA, DON'T YOU THINK THAT YOUR WORK IS JUST A TINY DROP COMPARED TO THE OCEAN OF POVERTY THROUGHOUT THE WORLD?

...YES, YOU'RE RIGHT. OUR WORK IS JUST A ...ROP. BUT IF OUR DROP WERE NOT THERE, THE MISERY WOULD BE ONE DROP MORE.

SO ... MOTHER TERESA, WHAT DO YOU THINK NEEDS TO CHANGE IN THE CHURCH TODAY?

YOU AND ME!

ON OCTOBER 17, 1979, MOTHER TERESA WAS AWARDED THE NOBEL PEACE PRIZE FOR HER DEDICATION TO SERVING THE POOREST OF THE POOR AROUND THE WORLD.

MOTHER TERESA SPENT THIRTY-FOUR YEARS TRAVELING. ON AVERAGE, SHE LEFT A HOUSE, COUNTRY, OR CONTINENT EVERY 2.6 DAYS!

WHAT TIME DO YOU HAVE TO BE AT THE VATICAN, MOTHER TERESA? I CAN DRIVE YOU.

EARLY MORNING!

FATHER LEO*, WE CAN'T BE LATE SO WE'LL LEAVE AT FOUR O'CLOCK..

HUH? FOUR IN THE MORNING?

PONTIFICAL GREGORIAN UNIVERSITY IN ROME

AT THE VATICAN

I TAKE IT THAT YOU'VE BEEN INVITED TO MORNING MASS WITH THE HOLY FATHER.

YES!

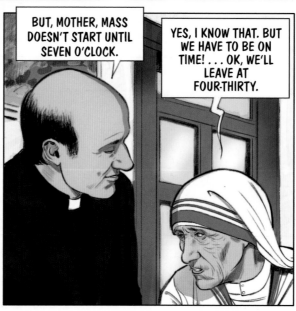

BUT, MOTHER, MASS DOESN'T START UNTIL SEVEN O'CLOCK.

YES, I KNOW THAT. BUT WE HAVE TO BE ON TIME! . . . OK, WE'LL LEAVE AT FOUR-THIRTY.

NO, MOTHER TERESA, THAT'S NOT NECESSARY. SIX-THIRTY IS EARLY ENOUGH.

OK, FATHER . . . FIVE O'CLOCK—BUT NO LATER!

THAT'S STILL MUCH TOO EARLY. THE VATICAN DOORS DON'T EVEN OPEN UNTIL SIX O'CLOCK.

OK, FATHER LEO . . . FIVE O'CLOCK, BUT NO LATER!

*Father Leo Maasburg traveled with Mother Teresa for seven years.

32

5:30 AM

6:00 AM

GOOD MORNING, MOTHER TERESA. YOU'RE TOO EARLY. PLEASE WAIT HERE.

THEN WE HAVE TIME TO PRAY A ROSARY . . .

HAIL, HOLY QUEEN, MOTHER OF MERCY, OUR LIFE, OUR SWEETNESS, AND OUR HOPE! TO YOU WE CRY, POOR BANISHED CHILDREN OF EVE; TO YOU WE SEND UP OUR SIGHS, MOURNING AND WEEPING IN THIS VALLEY OF TEARS. TURN THEN, MOST GRACIOUS ADVOCATE, YOUR EYES OF MERCY TOWARD US, AND AFTER THIS OUR EXILE, SHOW UNTO US THE BLESSED FRUIT OF YOUR WOMB, JESUS—

MOTHER TERESA, IT'S TIME.

I'LL WAIT HERE FOR YOU, MOTHER TERESA.

NO, FATHER LEO, YOU'RE COMING WITH US!

FATHER IS COMING WITH US!

I'M NOT ON THE VISITOR LIST, MOTHER. THEY'RE NOT GOING TO LET ME IN TO SEE THE HOLY FATHER.

YOU'RE COMING WITH US!

I THINK IT'S BETTER IF I WAIT FOR YOU IN THE CAR–

NO, FATHER LEO, YOU'RE WITH US.

FATHER LEO CONTINUED TO TRY TO CONVINCE MOTHER TERESA THAT HE SHOULD REMAIN BEHIND AS THEY WALKED DOWN THE LONG HALLWAY. SHE WOULD HAVE NONE OF IT.

GOOD MORNING, MOTHER TERESA. FATHER LEO IS NOT ON THE VISITOR LIST; HE CANNOT GO WITH YOU.

BUT HE'S WITH US.

I'M SORRY, MOTHER. HE DOES NOT HAVE PERMISSION TO ATTEND THIS MASS WITH HIS HOLINESS, POPE JOHN PAUL II.

WHO CAN GIVE US PERMISSION?

UHH . . . WELL . . . HMM . . . MAYBE THE POPE... OR BISHOP DZIWISZ.

GOOD. YOU WAIT HERE. . .

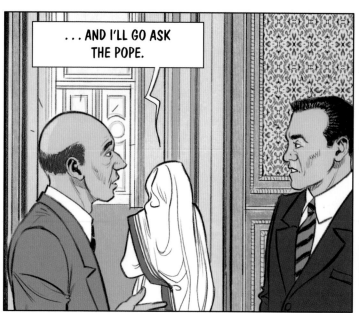

. . . AND I'LL GO ASK THE POPE.

MAMMA MIA! FOR THE LOVE OF GOD! MOTHER TERESA, JUST A MINUTE!

FINE! YOU WIN! FATHER LEO CAN GO WITH YOU.

EVEN THOUGH SHE WAS LESS THAN FIVE FEET TALL, MOTHER TERESA WAS KNOWN AS A FORCE TO BE RECKONED WITH.

BISHOP, EXCUSE ME. FATHER LEO WILL BE ABLE TO CONCELEBRATE WITH THE HOLY FATHER, WON'T HE?

OF COURSE HE MAY, MOTHER TERESA.

BISHOP DZIWISZ, THE HOLY FATHER'S SECRETARY, WASN'T SURPRISED THAT SHE HAD GOTTEN HER WAY. HE HAD KNOWN MOTHER TERESA FOR A LONG TIME.

SERVING THE POOR, EVEN IN THE AIR

MOTHER TERESA OFTEN FLEW ON PAN AMERICAN WORLD AIRWAYS FOR HER TRIPS. THE CREW CAME TO KNOW HER AND APPRECIATED HER PRESENCE AMONG THE PASSENGERS.

MOTHER TERESA, IT'S SUCH A JOY TO SEE YOU AGAIN! PLEASE LET ME TAKE YOU TO THE VIP LOUNGE AT NO CHARGE.

EVEN THOUGH SHE ALWAYS BOUGHT THE LEAST EXPENSIVE TICKETS, THE AIRLINE EMPLOYEES ALWAYS SAT HER IN BUSINESS CLASS.

MOTHER TERESA WAS GRATEFUL FOR THESE ACTS OF KINDNESS, BUT SHE NEVER EXPECTED OR DEMANDED THEM.

DO YOU THINK THAT I'LL HAVE A CHANCE TO SPEAK WITH MOTHER TERESA DURING THE FLIGHT?

UHM . . . , I'M NOT SURE. IT'S BEST IF YOU ASK HER IF SHE HAS TIME TO TALK.

OH, IT'S YOU! GOOD AFTERNOON. DID YOUR DAUGHTER FIND A JOB?

YOU REMEMBER ME, MOTHER TERESA?

OF COURSE, I REMEMBER YOU. HOW IS YOUR DAUGHTER?

SHE'S DOING MUCH BETTER SINCE SHE FOUND A JOB.

I'M GLAD! BY THE WAY I HAVE SOMETHING FOR HER . . .

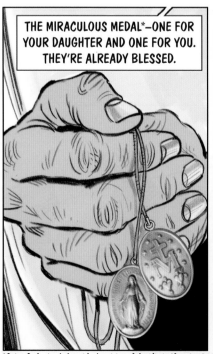

THE MIRACULOUS MEDAL*–ONE FOR YOUR DAUGHTER AND ONE FOR YOU. THEY'RE ALREADY BLESSED.

HOW KIND OF YOU! THANK YOU SO MUCH! MAY I BRING YOU SOMETHING TO EAT?

NO, THANK YOU. BUT IF IT'S POSSIBLE, AT THE END OF THE FLIGHT WE'D BE HAPPY TO TAKE ANY LEFTOVER FOOD FOR THE POOR.

*Saint Catherine Labouré had a vision of the Virgin Mary in 1840. The Blessed Mother told Saint Catherine to have a medal made to help the faithful ask for her intercession.

OFTEN MOTHER TERESA WAS SO EXHAUSTED FROM HER WORK THAT SHE NODDED OFF TO SLEEP DURING THE FLIGHT.

LADIES AND GENTLEMEN, MOTHER TERESA IS ON OUR FLIGHT TODAY. THE CREW HAS DECIDED TO TAKE UP A COLLECTION FOR HER WORK AMONG THE POOR.

TWO HOURS LATER . . .

WHILE YOU NAPPED, THE CREW COLLECTED $600 FOR YOUR MISSION.

HOW KIND! PERHAPS I SHOULD TAKE A NAP MORE OFTEN!

WARTIME RESCUE

BEIRUT, 1982–DURING THE CIVIL WAR IN LEBANON, CAREGIVERS FLED FROM AN ORPHANAGE FOR CHILDREN WITH SPECIAL NEEDS. THE CHILDREN WERE LEFT ALONE WITH NO ONE TO TAKE CARE OF THEM.

ABOUT FIFTY DISABLED CHILDREN ARE TRAPPED IN THIS BUILDING.

YES, RESCUING THE CHILDREN IS A GOOD IDEA, BUT THEY ARE IN THE MIDDLE OF ALL THE FIGHTING. WE CAN'T GO IN.

BUT WE MUST GO. I ASKED THE VIRGIN MARY TO GIVE US A CEASE-FIRE TOMORROW, THE DAY BEFORE THE FEAST OF HER ASSUMPTION INTO HEAVEN.

DO YOU HEAR THE BOMBS, MOTHER? I BELIEVE IN PRAYER BUT . . . IT'S IMPOSSIBLE!

TOMORROW THERE WI BE PEACE.

THE NEXT DAY

THERE'S A CEASE-FIRE! DON'T SHOOT!

FOR ONE DAY, THE WAR STOPPED. MOTHER TERESA HAD HER CHANCE.

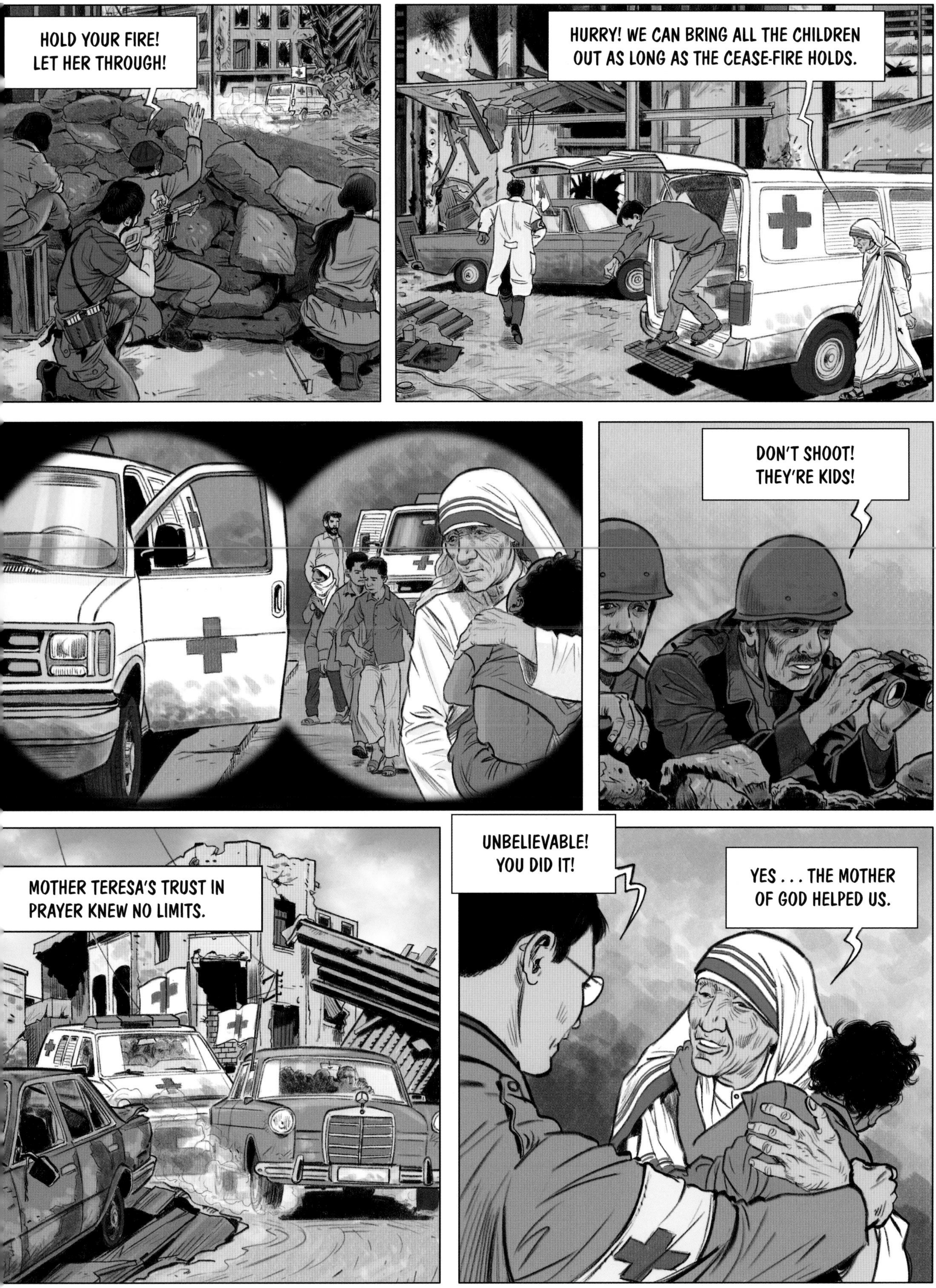
HOLD YOUR FIRE!
LET HER THROUGH!
HURRY! WE CAN BRING ALL THE CHILDREN OUT AS LONG AS THE CEASE-FIRE HOLDS.
DON'T SHOOT! THEY'RE KIDS!
MOTHER TERESA'S TRUST IN PRAYER KNEW NO LIMITS.
UNBELIEVABLE! YOU DID IT!
YES . . . THE MOTHER OF GOD HELPED US.

IN 1987, MOTHER TERESA SPENT A NIGHT IN MIAMI, FLORIDA.

A BUSINESS CARD

A MAN WAITED IN THE CAR FOR HIS WIFE. SHE HELPED THE SISTERS AS A VOLUNTEER.

MOTHER TERESA, I CAN FINALLY INTRODUCE YOU TO MY HUSBAND.

WHAT WORK DO YOU DO?

I'M AN ARCHITECT.

OH! SO YOU HAVE AN OFFICE! I'M SURE YOU'D BE ABLE TO MAKE ME SOME COPIES THEN.

I'D BE GLAD TO! COPIES OF WHAT?

MY BUSINESS CARD.

The fruit of silence is prayer.
The fruit of prayer is faith.
The fruit of faith is love.
The fruit of love is service.
The fruit of service is peace.

OK. HOW MANY WOULD YOU LIKE? TEN? TWENTY?

THIRTY THOUSAND . . .

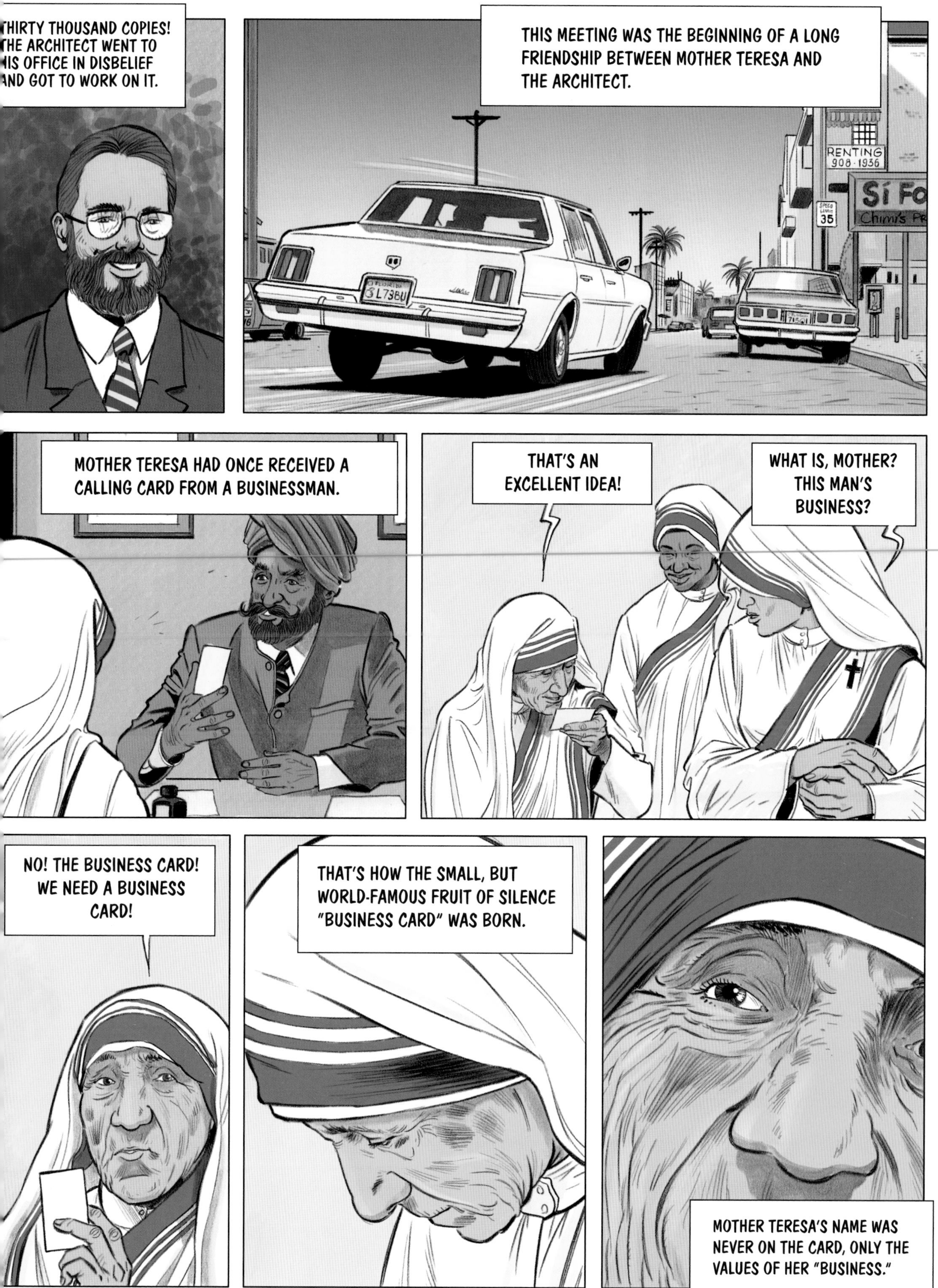
THIRTY THOUSAND COPIES! THE ARCHITECT WENT TO HIS OFFICE IN DISBELIEF AND GOT TO WORK ON IT.
THIS MEETING WAS THE BEGINNING OF A LONG FRIENDSHIP BETWEEN MOTHER TERESA AND THE ARCHITECT.
RENTING
908-1936
SPEED LIMIT
35
MOTHER TERESA HAD ONCE RECEIVED A CALLING CARD FROM A BUSINESSMAN.
THAT'S AN EXCELLENT IDEA!
WHAT IS, MOTHER? THIS MAN'S BUSINESS?
NO! THE BUSINESS CARD! WE NEED A BUSINESS CARD!
THAT'S HOW THE SMALL, BUT WORLD-FAMOUS FRUIT OF SILENCE "BUSINESS CARD" WAS BORN.
MOTHER TERESA'S NAME WAS NEVER ON THE CARD, ONLY THE VALUES OF HER "BUSINESS."

THE SISTERS OPENED A NEW HOUSE IN ZAGREB* AND MOTHER TERESA CAME TO VISIT THEM.

THE INITIALS "MC"

ZAGREB, 6:30AM

COULD YOU MAKE RESERVATIONS FOR A FLIGHT TO WARSAW, FATHER LEO? WE NEED TO FLY TO POLAND TODAY.

AT THIS TIME YUGOSLAVIA WAS A COMMUNIST COUNTRY WITH MANY RESTRICTIONS AND WIDESPREAD CORRUPTION.

10:15 AM

I HAVE THE TICKETS, MOTHER TERESA. WE DEPART AT THREE O'CLOCK.

I'M VERY SORRY, FATHER LEO, BUT WE AREN'T FLYING TO WARSAW AFTER ALL. WE HAVE TO GO TO MUNICH, GERMANY INSTEAD.

11:00 AM

12:50 PM

HERE, I WAS ABLE TO CHANGE THE TICKETS. YOU'RE VERY DISORGANIZED, THOUGH. IT'S TERRIBLE!

*Today, Zagreb is the capital of Croatia. At the time, Croatia was part of Yugoslavia.

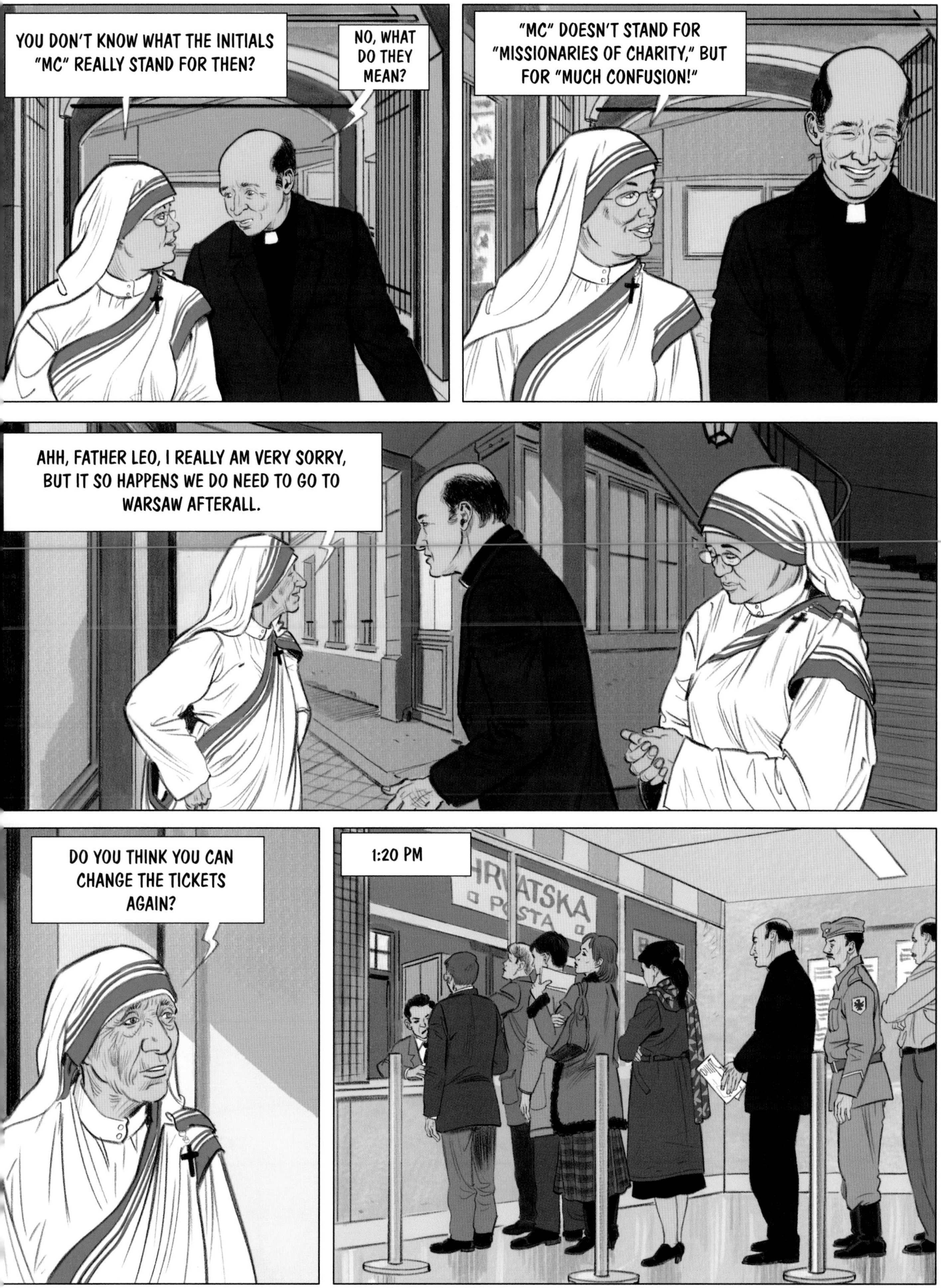
YOU DON'T KNOW WHAT THE INITIALS "MC" REALLY STAND FOR THEN?
NO, WHAT DO THEY MEAN?
"MC" DOESN'T STAND FOR "MISSIONARIES OF CHARITY," BUT FOR "MUCH CONFUSION!"
AHH, FATHER LEO, I REALLY AM VERY SORRY, BUT IT SO HAPPENS WE DO NEED TO GO TO WARSAW AFTERALL.
DO YOU THINK YOU CAN CHANGE THE TICKETS AGAIN?
1:20 PM
HRVATSKA POSTA

3:40 PM

HERE ARE THE TICKETS! WE HAVE JUST ENOUGH TIME TO DRIVE TO THE AIRPORT.

6:15 PM

MOTHER TERESA, TODAY I FOUND OUT FIRSTHAND THAT THE INITIALS "MC" REALLY STAND FOR "MUCH CONFUSION!"

BUT THAT'S ONLY ONE OF MANY POSSIBILITIES. "MC" ALSO STANDS FOR "MULTIPLE CHANGES" AND "MORE CONFUSION."

. . . AND BESIDES THAT THERE'S ALSO "MOTHER'S CRAZY!"

HAHAHA! STOP IT, MOTHER TERESA!

IN OCTOBER 1985, MOTHER TERESA WAS INVITED TO SPEAK AT THE UNITED NATIONS (UN) IN NEW YORK CITY.

A TYPICAL DAY

MOTHER TERESA BEGAN THIS DAY LIKE EVERY OTHER.

AFTER HOLY MASS, SHE SPENT AN HOUR OF ADORATION PRAYING BEFORE THE BLESSED SACRAMENT . . .

. . . AFTER THAT SHE WASHED SARIS . . .

. . . AND CLEANED THE FLOORS AND THE TOILETS.

"I'M A SPECIALIST IN TOILET CLEANING," MOTHER TERESA LIKED TO SAY.

AFTERWARD, SHE WAS DRIVEN THROUGH THE STREETS OF NEW YORK IN A RUSH.

WHEN SHE APPEARED AT THE UN, THIS "TOILET CLEANING SPECIALIST" WAS HAILED BY THE SECRETARY GENERAL, JAVIER PÉREZ DE CUÉLLAR, AS THE "MIGHTIEST WOMAN IN THE WORLD."

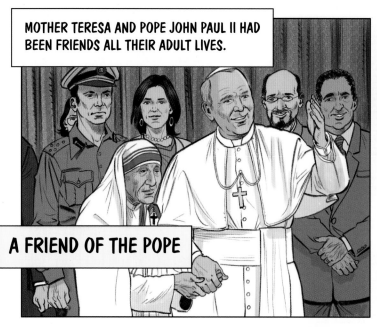

MOTHER TERESA AND POPE JOHN PAUL II HAD BEEN FRIENDS ALL THEIR ADULT LIVES.

A FRIEND OF THE POPE

THEY WERE BOTH AMONG THE LEADING FIGURES OF THE CHURCH AND THE WORLD IN THE TWENTIETH CENTURY.

BOTH HAVE ALSO BEEN PROCLAIMED SAINTS!

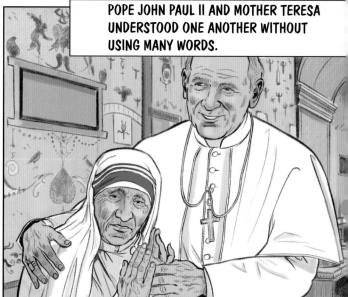

POPE JOHN PAUL II AND MOTHER TERESA UNDERSTOOD ONE ANOTHER WITHOUT USING MANY WORDS.

HOLY FATHER, WE NEED A PATRON SAINT FOR OUR LEPERS.

WHO ARE YOU THINKING OF?

FATHER DAMIEN DE VEUSTER. HE LIVED WITH THE LEPERS ON THE HAWAIIAN ISLAND OF MOLOKAI.

DO YOU KNOW FATHER DAMIEN?

YES, OF COURSE.

RUSH TO CANONIZATION*

GOOD. THEN WHAT ARE WE WAITING FOR? WHEN CAN YOU CANONIZE HIM?

POPE JOHN PAUL II KNEW MOTHER TERESA TOO WELL TO DEBATE THE ISSUE WITH HER.

HE SUGGESTED THAT SHE PRESENT HER REQUEST TO CARDINAL PALAZZINI, THE MAN IN CHARGE OF THE CHURCH'S PROCESS OF CANONIZATION.

GOOD AFTERNOON, YOUR EMINENCE.

CARDINAL PALAZZINI WAS KNOWN AT THE VATICAN FOR BEING VERY INTELLIGENT. HE WAS ALSO KNOWN FOR HAVING A VERY GOOD SENSE OF HUMOR.

THE HOLY FATHER SENT ME. WHAT CAN I DO FOR YOU, MOTHER TERESA?

YOUR EMINENCE, WE NEED A PATRON SAINT FOR OUR LEPERS.

WHO SHOULD THAT BE?

FATHER DAMIEN DE VEUSTER. DO YOU KNOW HIM?

YES, BUT THERE IS A SMALL PROBLEM. HIS PRAYERS HAVEN'T BEEN ANSWERED BY ANY MIRACLES YET.

ACCORDING TO CHURCH LAW, THREE MIRACLES ARE NEEDED FOR SOMEONE TO BE NAMED A SAINT.

*The official Church process for naming someone a saint

 YES, BUT THE BIBLE SAYS: "NO ONE HAS GREATER LOVE THAN THIS, TO LAY DOWN ONE'S LIFE FOR ONE'S FRIENDS."* THAT IS EXACTLY WHAT FATHER DAMIEN DID.

 ISN'T THE BIBLE ENOUGH FOR A CANONIZATION?

*John 15:13

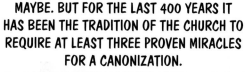 MAYBE. BUT FOR THE LAST 400 YEARS IT HAS BEEN THE TRADITION OF THE CHURCH TO REQUIRE AT LEAST THREE PROVEN MIRACLES FOR A CANONIZATION.

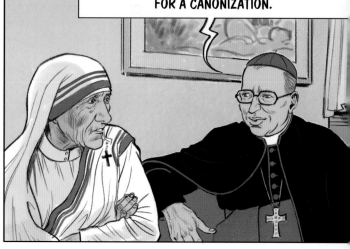

THEN THIS WOULD BE A GOOD OPPORTUNITY TO CHANGE THAT TRADITION.

PERHAPS, BUT DON'T YOU THINK IT WOULD BE SIMPLER TO ASK THE LORD FOR THE MIRACLES RATHER THAN CHANGE THE TRADITION?

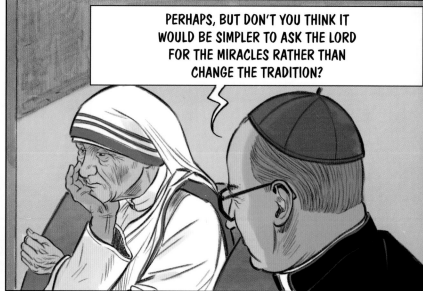

. . .

GOOD. WE'LL PRAY!

FIFTEEN YEARS LATER FATHER DAMIEN DE VEUSTER WAS PROCLAIMED A SAINT. DURING THAT TIME THE CHURCH CHANGED ITS TRADITION, AND NOW ONLY REQUIRES ONE MIRACLE FOR BEATIFICATION AND A SECOND MIRACLE FOR CANONIZATION.

MOTHER TERESA, THERE ARE SO MANY UNWANTED CHILDREN IN THIS HOSPITAL. WHAT WE CAN DO ABOUT IT?

SO MANY CHILDREN

MOTHER TERESA FOUND A DOCTOR WHO HELPED HER CARE FOR SOME ABANDONED CHILDREN.

GOOD, YOU CAN CHOOSE TWELVE CHILDREN. THERE ARE SOME WITH DISABILITIES AND OTHERS WHO HAVE NO CHANCE OF SURVIVAL.

THANK YOU! I'LL TAKE THOSE YOU THINK WILL DIE AND TRY TO HELP THEM.

MOTHER TERESA KNEW THAT EVERY CHILD IS A GIFT OF GOD.

LOOK AT HOW GENTLY HE HOLDS MY FINGER.

IF GOD CARES FOR US AS TENDERLY AS MOTHER TERESA CARES FOR THESE CHILDREN, THEN I CAN BE FULL OF HOPE.

ABORTION* IS WRONG. CHILDREN ARE A GIFT OF GOD. IF YOU DON'T WANT YOUR BABY, THEN GIVE THE CHILD TO ME. I WANT IT.

*Abortion ends the life of an unborn child during a mother's pregnancy. This violence was made legal in most countries during the twentieth century.

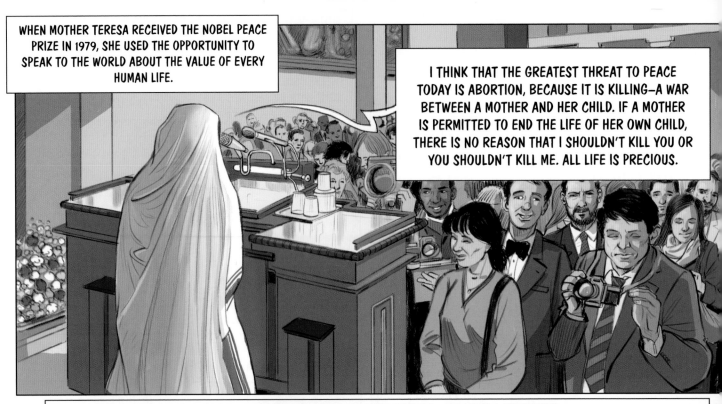

WHEN MOTHER TERESA RECEIVED THE NOBEL PEACE PRIZE IN 1979, SHE USED THE OPPORTUNITY TO SPEAK TO THE WORLD ABOUT THE VALUE OF EVERY HUMAN LIFE.

I THINK THAT THE GREATEST THREAT TO PEACE TODAY IS ABORTION, BECAUSE IT IS KILLING—A WAR BETWEEN A MOTHER AND HER CHILD. IF A MOTHER IS PERMITTED TO END THE LIFE OF HER OWN CHILD, THERE IS NO REASON THAT I SHOULDN'T KILL YOU OR YOU SHOULDN'T KILL ME. ALL LIFE IS PRECIOUS.

BECAUSE OF HER OPEN LOVE FOR UNBORN CHILDREN, MOTHER TERESA WAS OFTEN CRITICIZED.

Mother Teresa Pleas for a Stop to Abortion

MOTHER TERESA BEGS MOTHERS NOT TO ABORT THEIR CHILDREN . . .

YOUR SPEECH WAS BROADCAST OVER THE RADIO. YOUR WORDS HAVE MADE MANY WOMEN VERY ANGRY WITH THE CHURCH.

MY DEAR FATHER, JESUS SAID, "I AM THE TRUTH," AND IT'S OUR DUTY TO SPEAK THE TRUTH. IT'S THE CHOICE OF THOSE WHO HEAR IT TO ACCEPT IT OR REJECT IT.

TODAY, IN MANY DIFFERENT COUNTRIES UNWANTED CHILDREN ARE CARED FOR BY THE MISSIONARIES OF CHARITY.

I HAVE AIDS.* PLEASE TAKE MY BABY. I AM TOO SICK AND WEAK TO TAKE CARE OF HIM.

*AIDS is a life-threatening disease.

EPILOGUE: MOTHER TERESA AND THE POWER OF PRAYER

IN THE YEARS I, FATHER LEO, ACCOMPANIED MOTHER TERESA ON HER MANY TRIPS, I WAS ABLE TO WATCH THE WAY SHE BUILT SUCH AN ENORMOUS MINISTRY OF SERVICE THROUGHOUT THE WORLD. EVEN IN THE MOST DIFFICULT SITUATIONS, SHE WOULD FIND A WAY TO RECEIVE PERMISSION TO OPEN A HOUSE AND WORK THERE FOR THE POOREST OF THE POOR.

IT DIDN'T TAKE LONG BEFORE I NOTICED THAT THE WORKS MOTHER TERESA AND HER SISTERS DID CAME FROM THEIR DEEP FAITH. SHE KNEW THAT GOD ALONE HAD TO BE THE BUILDER. ONLY THEN WOULD THEIR WORK LAST. OFTEN SHE PRAYED, "JESUS, DESTROY WHAT I BUILD, UNLESS IT'S ACCORDING TO YOUR WILL."

ONE DAY A JOURNALIST FROM THE UNITED STATES ASKED MOTHER TERESA WHAT THE SECRET OF HER SUCCESS WAS. SHE ANSWERED HIM VERY SIMPLY: "I PRAY."

PRAYER WAS AS MUCH A PART OF MOTHER TERESA'S LIFE AS BREATHING WAS. WHEN SHE WASN'T DOING SOMETHING OR SPEAKING WITH SOMEONE, I WOULD SEE HER PRAYING. THE ROSARY WAS ALWAYS IN HER HANDS.

SHE HERSELF SAID, "I BELIEVE THERE ISN'T ANYONE WHO NEEDS GOD AS MUCH AS I DO. WITHOUT HIM, I AM SO USELESS AND WEAK. SINCE I CAN'T DEPEND ON MYSELF, I DEPEND ON GOD TWENTY-FOUR HOURS A DAY.

"MY SECRET IS SIMPLE: I PRAY. I LOVE PRAYER. THE DESIRE TO PRAY IS ALWAYS WITH ME. PRAYER MAKES YOUR HEART BIGGER UNTIL IT IS BIG ENOUGH TO HOLD THE GIFT OF GOD HIMSELF.

"MANY OF US WANT TO PRAY WELL, BUT THEN WE FAIL. IF YOU WANT TO PRAY BETTER, PRAY MORE. IF WE WANT TO BE ABLE TO LOVE, THEN WE MUST PRAY MORE."

THE MISSIONARIES OF CHARITY CONTINUE LIVING TODAY IN THIS SPIRIT OF PRAYER. EVERY DAY, THE SISTERS RECEIVE JESUS AT HOLY MASS. THEY ALSO SPEND AT LEAST ONE HOUR BEFORE THE BLESSED SACRAMENT, THE WAY MOTHER TERESA DID. FOR MOTHER TERESA, JESUS PRESENT IN THE EUCHARIST WAS THE SOURCE OF HER LIFE AND HER WORK.

IF ANYONE ASKED MOTHER TERESA HOW MANY HOUSES SHE HAD BUILT, SHE WOULD ANSWER, "WE'VE GIVEN JESUS THIS NUMBER OF TABERNACLES." SHE DID NOT SPEAK OF HOUSES, BUT OF TABERNACLES. THE PRESENCE OF JESUS WAS THE CENTER OF ALL SHE DID. MOTHER TERESA TIRELESSLY SOUGHT TO BRING JESUS TO ALL PEOPLE, AND ALL PEOPLE TO JESUS. SHE DID NOT ALLOW ANYTHING IN THE WORLD TO PREVENT HER FROM IGNITING A LIGHT FOR JESUS WHEREVER SHE WAS.

p. Leo

"Not all of us can do great things, but we can do small things with great love."

Prayer to Mother Teresa

Mother Teresa, you answered God's call to love him by serving the poorest of the poor. Because you saw Jesus in them, you spent your life loving the people we often ignore. Pray that God will help me to see those who are in need. And give me the grace to respond to their needs in love. Guide me in doing what I can, where I am . . . one person at a time. For like you, I believe that whatever I do for the least of my brothers and sisters I do for Christ. Amen.

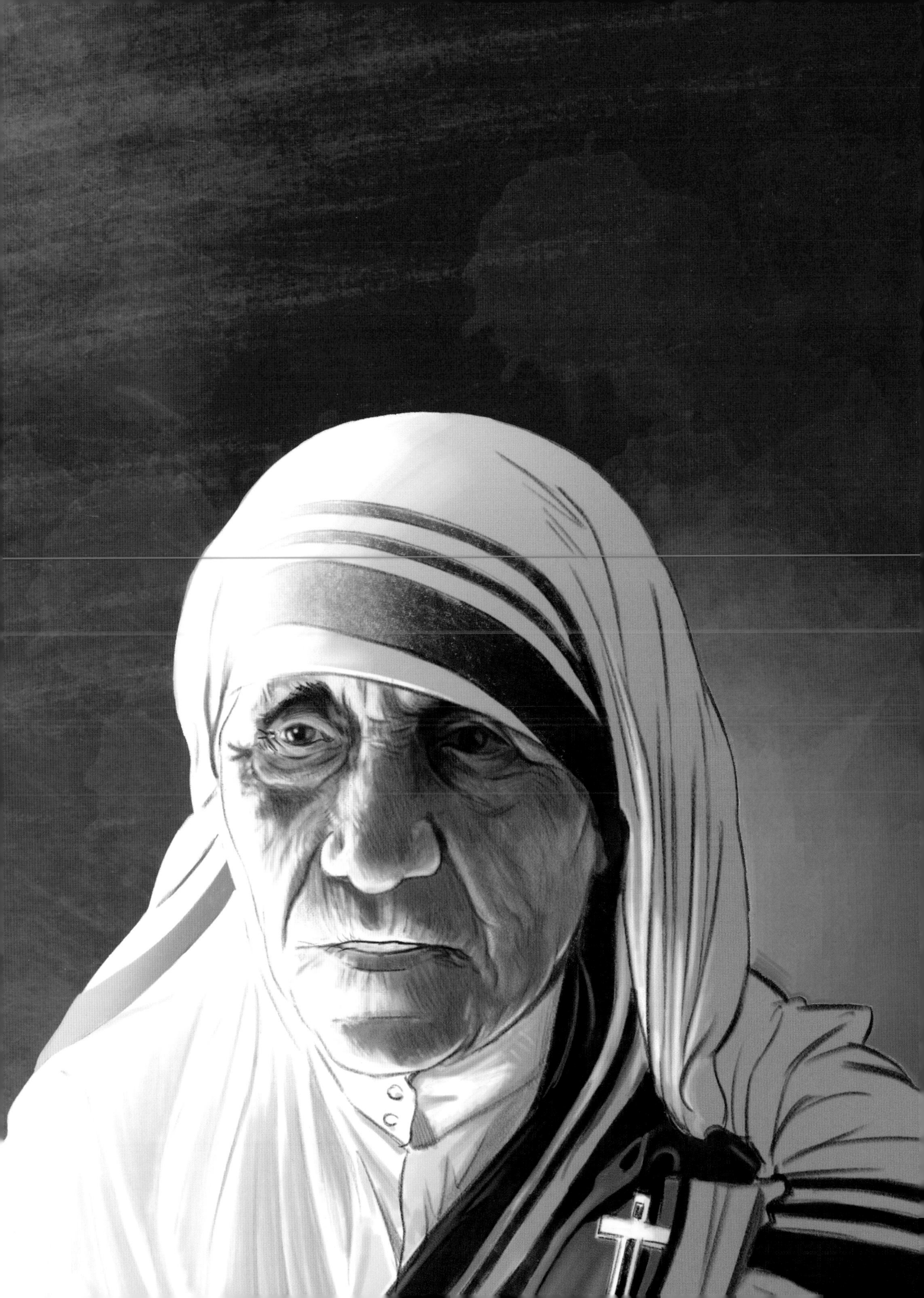

Courage
Commitment
Compassion

These are just some of the qualities of the saints you'll find in our popular Encounter the Saints series. Join Saint Teresa of Kolkata, Saint Thérèse of Lisieux, Saint John Paul II, and many other holy men and women as they discover and try to do what God asks of them. Get swept into the exciting and inspiring lives of the Church's heroes and heroines while encountering the saints in a new and fun way!

Collect all the
Encounter the Saints
books by visiting
www.pauline.org/
EncountertheSaints

Saint Teresa of Kolkata
Missionary of Charity
...lavich, SND

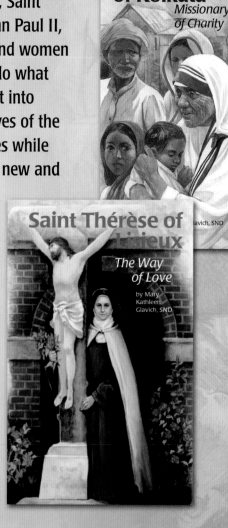

Saint Thérèse of ...sieux
The Way of Love
by Mary Kathleen Glavich, SND

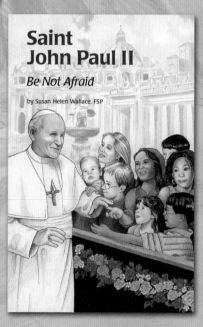

Saint John Paul II
Be Not Afraid
by Susan Helen Wallace, FSP

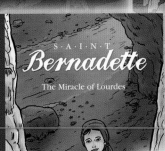

Pauline
BOOKS & MEDIA

The Daughters of St. Paul operate book and media centers at the following addresses. Visit, call, or write the one nearest you today, or find us at www.paulinestore.org.

CALIFORNIA
3908 Sepulveda Blvd, Culver City, CA 90230   310-397-8676
3250 Middlefield Road, Menlo Park, CA 94025   650-369-4230

FLORIDA
145 SW 107th Avenue, Miami, FL 33174   305-559-6715

HAWAII
1143 Bishop Street, Honolulu, HI 96813   808-521-2731

ILLINOIS
172 North Michigan Avenue, Chicago, IL 60601   312-346-4228

LOUISIANA
4403 Veterans Memorial Blvd, Metairie, LA 70006   504-887-7631

MASSACHUSETTS
885 Providence Hwy, Dedham, MA 02026   781-326-5385

MISSOURI
9804 Watson Road, St. Louis, MO 63126   314-965-3512

NEW YORK
64 West 38th Street, New York, NY 10018   212-754-1110

SOUTH CAROLINA
243 King Street, Charleston, SC 29401   843-577-0175

TEXAS
Currently no book center; for parish exhibits or outreach evangelization, contact: 210-569-0500 or SanAntonio@paulinemedia.com or P.O. Box 761416, San Antonio, TX 78245

VIRGINIA
1025 King Street, Alexandria, VA 22314   703-549-3806

CANADA
3022 Dufferin Street, Toronto, ON M6B 3T5   416-781-9131

SMILE GOD LOVES YOU!